Welcome to "Snack Attack: Healthy Recipes for Hungry Kids" cookbook! This book is filled with delicious and nutritious snack recipes that are perfect for kids who love to snack throughout the day.

We all know that kids love snacking, but it can be a challenge to find healthy options that they will actually enjoy. That's where this cookbook comes in! We've created a collection of easy-to-make snacks that are not only tasty, but also packed with nutrients that will keep kids fueled and focused throughout the day.

From sweet treats like fruit skewers with yogurt dip and energy balls, to savory options like hummus and veggie sticks and turkey roll-ups, there's something for every taste preference. The recipes are simple enough for kids to make on their own or with the help of an adult, and each recipe includes colorful pictures that will inspire even the pickiest eaters.

But this cookbook is more than just a collection of snack recipes. We've also included tips and tricks for healthy snacking, such as the importance of balanced meals and snacks, portion control, and how to make smart choices when snacking on the go. We believe that healthy snacking is not only important for kids' health and well-being, but also for their overall happiness and success.

We hope that this cookbook will inspire kids to get creative in the kitchen and to develop healthy snacking habits that will last a lifetime. So grab your apron, gather your ingredients, and let's get snacking!

Strawberry Muffins

Ingredients:

2 cups all purpose flour, spooned into measuring cup and leveled-off with knife, plus 2 teaspoons more for tossing with strawberries.
2 teaspoons baking powder.
¾ teaspoon salt.
1 stick or ½ cup unsalted butter, softened.
1 cup granulated sugar.
1½ teaspoons vanilla extract.
¼ teaspoon almond extract.

trawberry muffins are the perfect healthy snack for kids. Not only do they taste delicious, but they're also easy to make with just a few simple ingredients. Start by combining 2 cups of all purpose flour, 2 teaspoons baking powder, and ¾ teaspoon salt in a large bowl. Add 1 stick or ½ cup of softened unsalted butter, 1 cup of granulated sugar, 1½ teaspoons vanilla extract, and ¼ teaspoon almond extract. Using a hand mixer on a low setting, mix until the ingredients are just combined. Take 2 teaspoons of flour and toss it with ¾ to 1 cup of fresh strawberries that have been rinsed and dried. Gently fold the strawberry mixture into the muffin batter. Divide the batter evenly among 12 standard-size muffin cups and bake at 375 degrees for 20 minutes or until golden brown on top. Allow to cool before serving for healthy and delicious strawberry muffins your kids will love!

Enjoy!

Beet And Blueberry Pancakes

Ingredients
blueberries
1 medium beet, peeled and grated.
2 egg whites.
1 cup coconut milk.
1 tsp. pure vanilla extract.
1/4 cup sugar.
3/4 cup rice flour, all-puporse will work as well.
3/4 tsp. baking powder.
2 tsp. cinnamon.

This healthy snack is perfect for kids and easy to prepare. Start by pre-heating the oven to 350 degrees F. In a bowl, combine 1 cup of blueberries with the grated beet. Then, in a separate bowl, mix together the egg whites, coconut milk, vanilla extract and sugar until blended thoroughly. Next, add in the rice flour, baking powder and cinnamon; stir until all ingredients are fully combined. Finally fold the blueberry-beet mixture into the dough until evenly distributed throughout.

Using an 8x8 inch pan lined with parchment paper or greased lightly with oil , pour in the batter and spread it out evenly. Bake for 20 minutes or until golden brown on top. Serve hot or cold and enjoy!

Banana Muffins

Ingredients

1 and 1/2 cups (188g) all-purpose flour (spoon & leveled)
1 teaspoon baking powder.
1 teaspoon baking soda.
1/2 teaspoon salt.
1 teaspoon ground cinnamon.
1/4 teaspoon ground nutmeg.
3 large ripe bananas (about 1 and 1/2 cups mashed)*
6 Tablespoons (85g) unsalted butter, melted (or melted coconut oil)

Banana muffins are healthy snacks that the whole family can enjoy. Kids love them and they're easy to make! To get started, you'll need some basic ingredients. The first step is to preheat your oven to 350°F (177°C). Next, combine all of the dry ingredients in a medium bowl including 1 and 1/2 cups (188g) all-purpose flour, 1 teaspoon baking powder, 1 teaspoon baking soda, 1/2 teaspoon salt, 1 teaspoon ground cinnamon, and 1/4 teaspoon ground nutmeg. In a separate bowl mash 3 ripe bananas until smooth (about 1 and 1/2 cups mashed). Then add 6 Tablespoons (85g) melted butter or coconut oil. Stir together both mixtures until well combined.

Divide the batter evenly into 12 muffin tins and bake for 18-22 minutes, or until a toothpick inserted into the center of one comes out clean. Allow the muffins to cool before serving. Enjoy! Banana muffins make healthy snacks that kids will love and they're easy to prepare - perfect for breakfast, lunchboxes, or just as an afternoon treat!

Apple Nut Muffins

Ingredients:

2 cups all-purpose flour.
1/2 cup granulated sugar.
3 teaspoons baking powder.
1 1/2 teaspoon ground cinnamon, divided.
1/2 teaspoon salt.
2 eggs.
3/4 cup milk.
1 apple, peeled, cored, and finely chopped (about 1 cup)

These healthy snack muffins are a great way to get kids to enjoy healthy food. Not only are they easy to make, but they also have the added bonus of containing nutritious ingredients like apples, eggs and all-purpose flour.

To prepare these healthy snack muffins, start by preheating your oven to 375 degrees F. In a large bowl, whisk together the flour, sugar, baking powder, 1 teaspoon cinnamon and salt. In another bowl, beat together the eggs and milk until smooth. Then stir in the apple.

Next add the wet ingredients into the dry ingredients and mix until blended. Spoon the batter into greased or paper lined muffin cups filling them about two-thirds full. Sprinkle the remaining cinnamon over the top.

Bake for 18-20 minutes, or until a toothpick inserted into the center of the muffin comes out clean. Let cool before serving and enjoy! With these healthy snack muffins, your kids will love healthy food without even knowing it.

Happy snacking!

Yogurt Cereal Bars

ingredients

2 cups corn flakes 3/4 cup flour 1/4 cup brown sugar, firmly packed 1/2 teaspoon cinnamon 1/2 cup butter 1 cup yogurt, flavored 1 egg, slightly beaten 2 tablespoons flour

These healthy snacks are perfect for kids and easy to prepare. To make them, first preheat the oven to 350°F (177°C). In a medium bowl, mix together two cups of corn flakes, three-quarter cup of flour, a quarter cup of firmly packed brown sugar and half teaspoon of cinnamon. Melt the butter in the same bowl and then stir in one cup of flavored yogurt, one egg slightly beaten and two tablespoons of flour.

Once the ingredients are combined, spoon the mixture into greased muffin cups (or a greased muffin pan). Bake for 20 minutes or until golden brown. Let cool before serving. Enjoy!

Cheesy Slaty Sticks

Ingredients

250 g (2 cups) flour + some for the rolling.
250 g (~1 cup) butter, room temperature.
250 g (1 1/4 cups) cottage cheese.
pinch of salt.
1 egg.
150 g (or more) (1 1/2 cups) Gouda cheese.

Cheesy Salty Sticks are healthy snacks that kids love. Preparing them is easy and straightforward; all you need are a few ingredients and some free time. To begin, combine 250g of flour with 250g of butter at room temperature in a bowl. Make sure the mixture is even throughout the bowl before adding a pinch of salt and 250g of cottage cheese. Once everything is properly mixed, knead the dough until it becomes firm and you can form a ball. Place the dough in the fridge for about an hour, this will make it easier to work with later on.

Once the dough has cooled down, stretch it onto a lightly floured surface and roll out the dough with a rolling pin. Use a knife to cut the rolled-out dough into strips, and then use a cheese grater to grate 150g of Gouda cheese over the strips. Once you have added the cheese all over, fold each strip in half and twist it gently. Place the twisted strips on a baking sheet lined with parchment paper and brush them with a beaten egg. Bake your Cheesy Salty Sticks in the oven at 180°C (350°F) for about 15 minutes until they are golden brown and crispy. Enjoy!

Homemade Hummus

Homemade hummus is a healthy and delicious snack that kids of all ages will love. Preparing your own hummus at home isn't as intimidating as it may seem - with the right ingredients, it's actually quite easy to make.

To make homemade hummus, you'll need cooked chickpeas (dried or canned), tahini, extra-virgin olive oil, fresh lemon juice, garlic, water and sea salt. All of these ingredients can be found in most grocery stores, so you don't have to worry about tracking down anything hard to find.

To begin the hummus making process, simply place all of the ingredients into a food processor, and blend until you reach a creamy consistency. If you find that the hummus is too thick, add a tablespoon of water at a time to thin it out. Once you've reached your desired texture, season with salt to taste and enjoy!

Homemade hummus is perfect as an appetizer or healthy snack for kids.

Parmesan And Broccoli Muffins

Ingredients

☐ 2 tablespoons oil for greasing
☐ 240 grams flour 2 cups
☐ 3 teaspoons baking powder
☐ 1 medium egg
☐ ½ teaspoon salt
☐ ¼ teaspoon black pepper freshly crushed
☐ 240 milliliters milk 1 cup
☐ 60 milliliters vegetable oil ¼ cup or softened butter
☐ 1 broccoli head 1 ½ cups steamed and chopped small
☐ 200 grams cheddar cheese 2 cups, grated

Parmesan and Broccoli Muffins are healthy snacks that kids of all ages can enjoy. With just a few ingredients, these muffins can be prepared easily in no time. To get started, preheat the oven to 375°F (190°C). Grease a 12-cup muffin pan with oil or line it with cupcake liners.

In a large bowl, mix together the flour, baking powder, salt and pepper. In another bowl, lightly beat the egg with a fork and then stir in the milk and vegetable oil or butter until combined. Add the wet ingredients to the dry ingredients in the large bowl and stir just until blended.

Fold in the steamed and chopped broccoli and grated cheese. Spoon the batter into the prepared muffin cups, filling each one about two-thirds full. Bake until lightly golden brown, about 20 minutes. Let cool for at least 10 minutes before serving. Enjoy! These Parmesan and Broccoli Muffins make a great healthy snack for kids any time of the day. Enjoy!

Peanut Butter And Banana Sandwich

A peanut butter and banana sandwich is one of the healthiest snacks for kids. It's easy to make, healthy, and absolutely delicious! To prepare a peanut butter and banana sandwich, first gather all your ingredients: two slices of bread, some creamy peanut butter (you can also use crunchy if desired), and one ripe medium-sized banana. Begin by spreading the peanut butter on one slice of bread. Peel and slice the banana and arrange it onto the peanut butter-covered bread. Finally, top with the remaining piece of bread and press down lightly to make sure everything is secure. Enjoy your healthy snack! For an extra tasty treat, try adding some honey or cinnamon to the sandwich. You can also toast the sandwich in a toaster oven or panini press for a warm and crunchy treat. No matter how you prepare it, this classic peanut butter and banana sandwich is sure to please!

This healthy snack is very easy to make and perfect for little kids who want something sweet but healthy. Enjoy!

Cream Cheese And Egg Sandwich

Egg on Toast is an easy and healthy snack that kids of all ages will love. It's simple to prepare - just heat a skillet over medium heat, add butter, crack in the egg and cook for 3-4 minutes before flipping and cooking for 1-2 minutes more until the yolk is cooked through. Spread herby cream cheese on the toast and top with the cooked egg. Serve it up with an 8-ounce glass of milk as a healthy snack that your kids will love! With minimal effort, Egg on Toast is a perfect healthy treat for your little ones. Enjoy!

Strawberry Biscuits

Ingredients
☐ 1 ⅔ cups all purpose flour*
¼ cup granulated sugar.
1 tablespoon baking powder.
½ teaspoon kosher salt.
6 tablespoons cold unsalted butter, cut into about 20 pieces.
⅔ cup chopped fresh strawberries, about 6-8 strawberries.
⅔ cup cold buttermilk, plus more if needed.
¾ teaspoon pure vanilla extract.

Preheat the oven to 425°F and line a baking sheet with parchment paper. In a medium bowl, whisk together the all purpose flour, granulated sugar, baking powder and kosher salt. Add the cold butter pieces to the bowl and use a pastry blender or two knives to cut the butter into the flour mixture until it resembles coarse crumbs.

Stir in the chopped strawberries and then pour in the cold buttermilk and vanilla extract. Gently mix the ingredients together with a wooden spoon until just combined, being careful to not overmix.

Lightly flour a clean work surface and turn out the dough. Use your hands to shape it into an 8 inch circle, about one inch thick. Cut the dough into 8 equal wedges and place them on the prepared baking sheet.

Bake the biscuits for 15-20 minutes, or until golden brown. Let them cool for about 5 minutes before serving. Enjoy!

Banana Smothie

Banana smoothies are healthy snacks that kids will love. They are easy to prepare and you only need a few ingredients. All you need is 1 cup of sliced banana (frozen is best, about 1 large banana), ¼ cup Greek yogurt (plain or vanilla), ¼ cup milk (dairy, almond, oat milk, etc.), and ¼ teaspoon vanilla extract. To make the smoothie, simply blend all of the ingredients until it's creamy and smooth. You can also add honey if desired for a sweeter flavor. Enjoy this healthy treat as a snack in-between meals or after exercise! It's sure to be a hit with your little ones!

For a fun twist, try adding different healthy ingredients to the smoothie such as chia seeds, flaxseeds, unsweetened coconut flakes or even a handful of spinach. Whatever your kids enjoy will work great! Serve with some homemade granola for an extra special treat that's healthy and delicious.

The possibilities are endless when it comes to healthy snacks and banana smoothies are just one option. There are many other healthy snacks you can prepare for your family. Start exploring today and create healthy treats everyone in your family will enjoy!

Oatmeal Cookies

Ingredients

1 1/2 cups (212g) all-purpose flour (scoop and level to measure)
1 tsp ground cinnamon.
1 cup (226g) unsalted butter, softened slightly (it should still be somewhat cold and firm)
1 cup (200g) packed light brown sugar.
1/2 cup (100g) granulated sugar.
1 1/2 tsp vanilla extract.

Begin by preheating the oven to 350°F. Next, cream together the softened butter and both sugars until light and fluffy. Beat in the vanilla extract, then gradually add in the flour and cinnamon until fully combined.

Scoop out about two tablespoons of cookie dough for each cookie and place on a parchment-lined baking sheet, leaving enough room between each one for them to spread. Bake for 10 to 12 minutes until golden brown, then let cool before enjoying your homemade oatmeal cookies! Enjoy these healthy snacks with your family or friends - they're sure to love them!

That's it - a simple and delicious recipe for healthy oatmeal cookies that kids of all ages can enjoy. With just a few ingredients, you can whip up this treat in no time. So, get baking and start enjoying your homemade oatmeal cookies! Happy snacking!

Green Smoothie

Tired of kids asking for unhealthy snacks? Want to give them something healthy and fun? Look no further than this delicious smoothie recipe! It's a great way to get in some leafy greens as well as healthy fruits, like mango, pineapple and banana. Plus it only takes minutes to prepare.

Start by tightly packing two cups of leafy greens into a measuring cup. Then, toss the greens into a blender with some water and blend until there are no more leafy chunks. Next, add in mango, pineapple and bananas for a healthy dose of nutrients. Blend everything together again until it becomes smooth.

Lastly, pour the delicious smoothie into a mason jar (or your favorite cup) and watch the kids enjoy healthy snacks. They'll be feeling like rawkstars!

Try this healthy smoothie recipe today, and make sure to get creative with your ingredients. Enjoy!

Sweet Potato Fries

Sweet potatoes make healthy snacks for kids and their preparation is simple. To get started, mix together the spices, salt and pepper in a small bowl. Toss this mixture with the sweet potatoes to coat them evenly. Spread out the potatoes on two rimmed baking sheets and bake until brown and crisp on one side, about 15 minutes. Flip them over and bake until the other side is crisp, which takes about 10 minutes. Serve the sweet potatoes hot as healthy snacks for kids. Enjoy!

Homemade Veggie Chips

Veggie chips are a healthy and delicious snack option for kids. They can be easily prepared at home in your own kitchen with minimal ingredients and effort. A combination of root vegetables, starchy vegetables, salt and pepper, and cooking spray is all you need to make veggie chips that are healthy and flavorful.

To start off, you'll need to preheat your oven to 375 degrees Fahrenheit. Wash and dry the carrots, beetroot, and zucchini. Slice them thinly into rounds or sticks - whatever shape you prefer! Then spread them out on a baking sheet lined with parchment paper. Drizzle a little bit of cooking spray over the vegetables to ensure even crispiness and add salt and pepper to taste.

Once all the vegetables are on the baking sheet, pop it into the preheated oven for about 10-15 minutes. Keep an eye on them so that they don't overcook - you want to achieve a crisp outer texture without burning the veggies! Once your veggie chips are done cooking, let them cool before serving.

Veggie chips are a healthy and tasty snack that the whole family can enjoy. They're quick and easy to make, so why not give them a try? Your kids will love this healthy alternative to store-bought snacks - plus, you know exactly what goes into it! Enjoy!

Cheese Crackers

Ingredients

6 ounces sharp yellow cheddar cheese, shredded (1 and 1/2 cups shredded)*
1 cup (125g) all-purpose flour (spoon & leveled)
1 and 1/2 teaspoons cornstarch*
1/4 teaspoon salt
6 Tablespoons (85g) unsalted butter, cold and cut into 6 pieces
2 Tablespoons cold water
optional: sea salt for sprinkling

Cheese crackers are healthy snacks that kids love. They are packed with protein, calcium, and healthy fats from the cheese and butter. Making them at home is easy too--all you need is a few simple ingredients!

To make your own cheese crackers start by combining the flour, cornstarch and salt in a medium bowl. Use a whisk to mix it all together. Then add your shredded cheese and stir until it's fully combined into the dry mixture. Now cut in the cold butter pieces using either a pastry cutter or fork until the mixture resembles coarse crumbs (it should look like wet sand when you're done). Finally add one tablespoon of cold water at a time while stirring with a wooden spoon until everything comes together in a ball.

Once your dough is ready, roll it out onto parchment paper or a lightly floured surface to about 1/8-inch thickness. Cut into desired shapes and place them on an ungreased baking sheet. Sprinkle with sea salt if desired and bake at 350°F (177°C) for 18-20 minutes or until golden brown. Enjoy these healthy cheese crackers as an afternoon snack!

Avocado Toast

Ingredients
for avocado toast
2large slices crusty, chewy sourdough bread, preferably whole wheat.
1ripe avocado, halved, pit removed.
Extra-virgin olive oil.
Flaky salt and coarsely ground black pepper.
Half a lemon or lime.

Avocado toast is an healthy and delicious snack for kids that's both nutritious and simple to prepare. To make it, you'll need two slices of crusty sourdough bread, preferably whole wheat; one ripe avocado, halved with the pit removed; extra-virgin olive oil; a pinch of flaky salt, coarsely ground black pepper, and half a lemon or lime.

To start prepping, toast your bread slices until lightly golden brown - this will add an extra crunch to your avocado toast. Once the bread has cooled slightly, spread each slice with mashed avocado and season with salt, pepper and a squeeze of citrus juice. Finally, drizzle generously with extra- virgin olive oil before serving. Enjoy!

Healthy Donuts

For healthy donuts that kids will love, why not try these healthy-yet-delicious alternatives? Using self rising flour, maple syrup, coconut oil and the milk of your choice, you can create healthy sweet treats in no time.

Start by preheating the oven to 350°F (175°C). In a medium bowl, mix together all the dry ingredients: 1 cup self-rising flour, 1/2 teaspoon baking powder, and 2 tablespoons of dark cocoa powder or cacao powder. Mix until everything is evenly distributed.

Next, melt 4 tablespoons of coconut oil in a small saucepan. Once melted completely, remove from heat and pour over the dry ingredients in the bowl. Then add in 1/3 cup maple syrup, and mix until everything is combined.

Finally, pour in the milk of your choice to create a dough-like consistency. Grease a donut pan with oil or butter and fill each cavity with the healthy donut dough. Place in the preheated oven for about 10 minutes or until golden brown. Let cool before serving and enjoy!

These healthy donuts make an ideal snack for kids who are looking for something sweet but healthy at the same time. They can even help prepare these healthy snacks themselves! With this easy recipe, healthy snacking has never been easier or more delicious!

Carrot Cake

Carrot cake is a delicious healthy snack for kids that can be prepared easily in no time. With the combination of just the right ingredients, you can make this scrumptious dessert at home. You will need 2 cups (260g) chopped pecans - 1 cup for cake and 1 cup for garnish, 1 and 1/2 cups (300g) packed light or dark brown sugar, 1/2 cup (100g) granulated sugar, 1 cup (240ml) vegetable oil or canola oil (or melted coconut oil)*, 4 large eggs, 3/4 cup (133g) smooth unsweetened applesauce and 1 teaspoon pure vanilla extract to prepare carrot cake.

To start preparing the carrot cake, mix all the dry ingredients together in a bowl - chopped pecans, brown sugar, granulated sugar and applesauce. In another bowl, add the eggs and beat them until they are light and fluffy. Then pour in the vegetable oil or canola oil. Add the vanilla extract to this mixture as well.

Once you have both bowls ready with their respective mixtures, combine them together and stir until everything is evenly mixed. Grease a 10" round cake pan with butter or non-stick cooking spray before pouring your batter into it. Bake at 350°F (176°C) for about 25-35 minutes or until an inserted toothpick comes out clean.

Let your healthy carrot cake cool before garnishing it with the remaining cup of chopped pecans. This healthy snack for kids will surely make them happy and healthy! Enjoy!

Note: If you are using coconut oil, melt it first before pouring into the mixture.

Tuna Sandwich

Tuna sandwiches are a healthy and tasty snack option for kids. Preparing this classic sandwich is quite simple - all you need are some canned tuna, mayonnaise, hard cooked egg, lemon juice, celery, sweet pickle relish and lemon pepper seasoning.

To get started, open the cans of chunk light or albacore white tuna (if using cans) and drain the liquid prior to use. Then mix together the mayonnaise with the chopped egg, lemon juice, celery, sweet pickle relish and lemon pepper seasoning in a bowl. Once everything is mixed well together it's time to assemble your sandwich! Start by layering lettuce leaves on two slices of bread then top with the tuna mixture. Finally, top the sandwich with the other two slices of bread and cut in half.

Tuna sandwiches are a healthy snack for kids that can be prepared quickly and easily. Enjoy!

Note: If using pouches instead of canned tuna, flake the tuna with a fork before mixing with the other ingredients. It's also important to store any remaining sandwich mixture in an airtight container in the refrigerator. Consume within 1-2 days for best results.

Blueberry Waffles

Blueberry waffles are a healthy and delicious snack for kids. They can be enjoyed for breakfast, a mid-afternoon snack, or even as a dessert. Preparing blueberry waffles is relatively simple and requires only seven ingredients: 3 egg yolks, 1 ⅔ cups milk, 2 cups all-purpose flour, 2 ¼ teaspoons baking powder, ½ teaspoon salt, ¼ cup melted butter, 3 egg whites (stiffly beaten), and ⅔ cup blueberries.

Begin by preheating your waffle iron to the desired temperature. In a medium bowl whisk together the egg yolks and milk until combined. Add in the flour, baking powder and salt until just evenly incorporated – don't over mix. In a separate bowl, beat the egg whites until stiff peaks form. Then slowly fold in the egg whites into the other mixture and stir just until combined.

Finally, fold in melted butter and blueberries into your batter. Grease your waffle iron lightly with butter or cooking spray then spoon out some of the batter onto the hot waffle iron and cook according to instructions. Serve warm with toppings like fresh fruit, syrup or powdered sugar for healthy snacks that kids will love! Enjoy!

Peanut Butter Cookies

Peanut butter cookies are a healthy snack option for kids that can be whipped up in no time! To make these delicious treats, you will need the following ingredients: 1 cup of unsalted butter (Great Value Sweet Cream Unsalted Butter, 16 oz.), 1 cup of crunchy peanut butter, 1 cup white sugar, 1 cup packed brown sugar, 2 large eggs, 2 ½ cups all-purpose flour, 1 ½ teaspoons baking soda and 1 teaspoon baking powder.

To start the preparation process preheat the oven to 375 degrees Fahrenheit. Next cream the butter and both sugars together until light and fluffy. Once combined add the eggs one at a time followed by the peanut butter. In a separate bowl mix together the dry ingredients, then slowly add the dry ingredients to the wet mixture and stir until combined.

Once you have all of your ingredients mixed together, roll the dough into 1 inch balls and flatten with a fork. Place the cookies on an ungreased baking sheet, making sure they are spaced 2-3 inches apart. Bake in preheated oven for 8-10 minutes or until lightly golden brown. Let cool completely before serving as healthy snacks for kids! Enjoy!

Strawberry Toast

Strawberry Toast is a healthy and tasty breakfast option for kids that's easy to prepare. To make it, start by melting the butter in a medium-sized skillet over medium heat. Add the sliced strawberries and cook for 5 minutes or until the berries have softened. Next, add the maple syrup, orange zest, non-fat milk, and teaspoon of salt. Cook for another 3 minutes or until the mixture thickens. Finally, place the slices of cinnamon raisin bread in a single layer on top of the strawberry mixture. Crack three eggs over the toast and let cook until the whites are set and yolks have just started to become soft. Serve immediately with a sprinkle of extra orange zest. Enjoy!

Egg Muffins

When it comes to baking, there are many options to choose from that will tantalize your taste buds. From cakes and cupcakes, to muffins and brownies, there's something for everyone. But one of the most popular treats is the classic egg muffin. Egg muffins are quick and easy to make and perfect for breakfast on-the-go. Here's what you'll need:

- Eggs
- Milk
- Cheese
- Veggies of your choice (onion, bell peppers, mushrooms, spinach are all great options)
- Butter or oil for cooking
- Salt and pepper to taste.

Start by preheating the oven to 375 degrees F and greasing a muffin pan with butter or oil. In a large bowl, whisk together eggs, milk, cheese and veggies. Fill each muffin cup about 3/4 full with egg mixture and season with salt and pepper to taste. Bake for 25 minutes or until egg is set. Enjoy! With egg muffins you can have a delicious breakfast ready in no time

Cocoa Cake

c

Ingredients: 2 cups (240g) all-purpose flour. 3/4 cup (64g) unsweetened cocoa powder. 1 & 1/4 teaspoons baking soda. 3/4 teaspoon salt. 3/4 cup (170g) unsalted butter, softened. 1 & 3/4 cups (350g) firmly packed light brown sugar. 2 large eggs. 1 & 1/3 cups (314ml) water.

To make the cocoa cake, start by preheating the oven to 350°F (177°C). Grease and flour a 9 x 13-inch baking pan. In a medium bowl, whisk together the all-purpose flour, cocoa powder, baking soda and salt until evenly combined. In a large bowl using an electric mixer on medium speed, cream together the butter and brown sugar until light and fluffy. Add in the eggs one at a time, beating well after each addition. Gradually add in the dry ingredients in three batches alternately with water in two batches until just combined. Pour into prepared pan and bake for about 40 minutes or until toothpick inserted into center comes out clean. Allow cake to cool completely before serving. Enjoy

Chia Budding

Ingredients

1 14 ounce can unsweetened light coconut milk.
1 cup plain fat-free Greek yogurt.
2 tablespoon pure maple syrup.
½ teaspoon vanilla.
¼ cup chia seeds.
2 cup chopped fresh fruit or berries, such as pineapple, strawberries, blueberries, raspberries, mango, and/or peach)

Chia budding is a healthy and easy breakfast that can be prepared quickly. It's perfect for busy parents who want to give their kids a healthy start to the day. To prepare chia budding, you'll need 1 14 ounce can of unsweetened light coconut milk, 1 cup of plain fat-free Greek yogurt, 2 tablespoons of pure maple syrup, ½ teaspoon of vanilla extract and ¼ cup of chia seeds. Combine the ingredients in a bowl until everything is thoroughly mixed together. Then add the chopped fresh fruit or berries - such as pineapple, strawberries, blueberries, raspberries, mango and/or peach - and stir again until everything is evenly distributed. Spoon the mixture into individual serving dishes, cover, and refrigerate overnight. In the morning, your chia pudding will be ready to enjoy! It's a healthy and delicious breakfast that both kids and adults can enjoy. Enjoy!

!

Banana Baked Oatmeal

Ingredients: 2 cups rolled oats. ½ cup pecan pieces (optional) 1 teaspoon baking powder. 1 ½ teaspoons cinnamon. ½ teaspoon allspice. ½ teaspoon kosher salt. ¾ cup mashed banana or 2 very ripe bananas. 1 ¾ cups milk of choice (dairy, almond or oat)

If you're looking for something warm and healthy to make your kids in the morning, try banana baked oatmeal! Start by preheating the oven to 350F (180C). In a bowl, mix together the rolled oats, pecan pieces (optional), baking powder, cinnamon, allspice and salt. Add in mashed banana or two very ripe bananas and milk of choice (dairy, almond or oat) and stir until everything is combined. Spread this mixture into an 8x8 inch baking dish and bake for 35 minutes. Let cool before serving. This delicious breakfast option can be served with yogurt or fruit for an extra healthy boost! Kids will love it!

Apple Muffins

With just a few simple ingredients, you can make healthy apple muffins that are perfect for a quick breakfast or snack. Whether you're feeding kids or just looking for an easy-to-make healthy treat, these muffins are sure to be a hit! To prepare the apple muffins, begin by preheating your oven to 350 degrees Fahrenheit. In a large bowl, combine 2 cups of sugar, 2 eggs, and 1 cup of oil like vegetable, canola, or coconut oil. Then add in 1 tablespoon of vanilla extract. In a separate bowl mix together 3 cups all-purpose flour with 1 teaspoon each of salt, baking soda, and cinnamon. Gradually stir the dry ingredients into the wet ones until both are fully combined. Fold in 2 cups of diced apples, then spoon the muffin batter into greased or paper-lined muffin tins. Bake the muffins on the center rack in your preheated 350 degree oven for 20 to 25 minutes or until a wooden toothpick inserted into the center comes out clean. Let the muffins cool on a wire cooling rack before serving and enjoy! The healthy apple muffins are great as a quick breakfast option for kids or as an afternoon snack. They're also delicious served warm with a pat of butter or cream cheese. Make sure to store any leftover muffins in an airtight container at room temperature for up to 4 days. Enjoy!

Banana Bread

Banana bread is a healthy and delicious breakfast option for kids. It is filled with energy-boosting healthy ingredients like ripe bananas, flour, sugar, salt, baking soda, vanilla extract and softened butter. If you want to make it an even heartier and more flavorful meal, you can also add walnuts and raisins to turn it into banana nut bread.

Making banana bread is easy! Start by preheating your oven to 350 degrees Fahrenheit. In one bowl mix together the dry ingredients - flour, sugar, salt and baking soda - until they are well combined. In another bowl mash the ripe bananas until smooth then stir in softened butter, eggs and vanilla extract until everything is fully incorporated. Combine the wet ingredients with the dry ingredients and fold together. Lastly, if desired, mix in walnuts and raisins.

Once everything is blended, pour the batter into a greased loaf pan and bake for 50-60 minutes or until a toothpick inserted into the middle comes out clean. Serve warm with butter or cream cheese - enjoy!

Banana bread makes a healthy breakfast for kids that is sure to please everyone in the family. Try making it today for an easy and healthy start to any day!

Smoked Salmon Toast

Ingredients : 1 ripe avocado. 1 tablespoon crème fraîche. 1 lemon. 70 g radishes. 3 sprigs of fresh dill. 1 tablespoon cider vinegar. 12-16 slices of crispbread or thinly sliced and toasted rye bread. 200 g smoked salmon , from sustainable sources.

Smoked Salmon Toast is a healthy and delicious breakfast option for kids. It's easy to prepare, with just a few simple ingredients - ripe avocado, crème fraîche, lemon, radishes, fresh dill, cider vinegar, crispbread or thinly sliced and toasted rye bread and smoked salmon.

To make the toast: Start by slicing the avocado into thin slices and arranging them on top of the toast. Mix together the crème fraîche with some freshly squeezed lemon juice until combined. Spread this mixture over the avocado slices. Slice the radishes into thin rounds and arrange them around each slice of toast. Sprinkle some finely chopped dill onto each slice of toast. Drizzle over some cider vinegar and top with some smoked salmon.

Serve the Smoked Salmon Toast for a healthy and delicious breakfast for kids. Enjoy!

Cottage Cheese Pancakes

Ingredients
1 1/2 cups cottage cheese
4 eggs
1 tsp vanilla extract
2 tbsp sugar
1 tbsp baking powder
1 cup flour
1/4 cup canola oil

To begin making your cottage cheese pancakes, whisk together the cottage cheese and eggs until all the lumps are gone. Then add in the vanilla extract, sugar, baking powder and flour. Whisk until everything is well incorporated. Finally add in the canola oil and mix until combined. Heat a skillet to medium heat and pour 1/4 cup of the batter onto the pan. Cook until small bubbles start to form around the edge, then carefully flip over with a spatula and cook for another 2-3 minutes. Serve your cottage cheese pancakes hot with butter or syrup. Enjoy! These healthy pancakes are sure to provide your kids with the energy they need for their busy days ahead. You can even add in some fruit, nuts or chocolate chips for an extra special treat! With just a few simple steps you can have a healthy breakfast ready in no time. Give them a try today!

Pecan Energy Bars

Pecan energy bars make an excellent healthy breakfast for kids. This quick and easy snack is prepared in a few simple steps: 1. Pit the dates and place them in a food processor, adding the pecans, oats, chia seeds, vanilla extract, cinnamon and salt. Pulse until everything is combined into a thick paste. 2. Line a baking dish with parchment paper and press the mixture into it evenly, making sure that all the edges are sealed. 3. Refrigerate for two hours or until set, then cut into bars and enjoy! Store any extra energy bars in an airtight container in the refrigerator for up to one week. Pecan energy bars make a healthy, nutritious breakfast for kids that will jump-start their day with healthy ingredients like dates, pecans and oats. Enjoy!

Blueberry Smoothie

A healthy breakfast is essential for providing energy and nutrients needed to fuel a busy day of activities, especially for growing kids. A blueberry smoothie is an ideal way for children to get the nutrition they need in a tasty, quick way. This recipe calls for just five ingredients and takes only five minutes to prepare. Start by gathering the necessary ingredients: 1 cup blueberries (frozen or fresh), 1 container plain yogurt, ¾ cup 2% reduced-fat milk, 2 tablespoons white sugar, ½ teaspoon vanilla extract and ⅛ teaspoon ground nutmeg. You can buy all these items at your local grocery store or online. Blend together all of these ingredients until the mixture is smooth and creamy. If you want to make it extra healthy, substitute the reduced-fat milk with almond or soy milk. You can also use honey instead of white sugar if you prefer a less sweet smoothie. For an added twist, consider adding other healthy ingredients like kale, spinach, banana or chia seeds - just remember to adjust the liquid levels accordingly. Serve in tall glasses and enjoy! With these simple steps, you can prepare a healthy and delicious breakfast for your kids in no time. The blueberry smoothie is a healthy and tasty way for children to get their daily dose of vitamins and minerals. With its sweet flavour and creamy texture, this refreshing drink will become your household's go-to morning treat!

I want to take a moment to express my heartfelt gratitude for your recent purchase of my recipe book. As a passionate food lover, nothing makes me happier than sharing my favorite recipes with others. Your decision to invest in my book not only supports my dream, but also shows your commitment to expanding your culinary horizons.

I sincerely hope that the recipes in the book will inspire you to try new things and add some excitement to your meals.

Thank you again for your support and for being a part of this journey with me. I hope my book will bring you many happy and delicious moments in the kitchen.

www.ingramcontent.com/pod-product-compliance
Lightning Source LLC
Chambersburg PA
CBHW041150110526
44590CB00027B/4179